War

MASSACHUSETTS

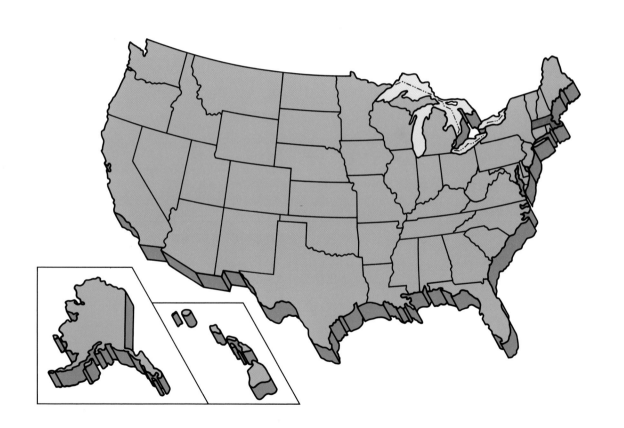

MASSACHUSETTS

J. F. Warner

Lerner Publications Company

This book is available in two editions:
Library binding by Lerner Publications Company
Soft cover by First Avenue Editions
241 First Avenue North
Minneapolis, MN 55401
ISBN: 0-8225-2737-5 (lib. bdg.)
ISBN: 0-8225-9666-0 (pbk.)

LIBRARY OF CONGRESS
CATALOGING-IN-PUBLICATION DATA
Warner, Jack.
   Massachusetts / by Jack Warner.
     p. cm. — (Hello USA)
   Includes index.
   ISBN 0-8225-2737-5 (lib. bdg.)
   1. Massachusetts—Juvenile literature.
   [1. Massachusetts.] I. Title. II. Series.
F64.3.W37 1994   93-37203
974.4—dc20   CIP
                      AC

Manufactured in the United States of America

1 2 3 4 5 6 - I/JR - 99 98 97 96 95 94

Cover photograph by
Tony La Gruth.

The glossary that begins on
page 68 gives definitions of
words shown in **bold type** in
the text.

 This book is printed
on acid-free, recycla-
ble paper.

CONTENTS

James Naismith, a physical education teacher, holds one of the first basketballs.

6

Did You Know . . . ?

❑ A small lake in Massachusetts has the longest name of any place in the country. Webster Lake's original Nipmuc Indian name is Chargoggagoggmanchaugagogg-chaubunagungamaug, which means "You fish on your side of the lake, I fish on my side, and no one fishes in the middle."

❑ Two popular sports had their beginnings in Massachusetts. In 1891 James Naismith of Springfield invented basketball, creating a team sport that could be played indoors during the winter. In 1895 William Morgan of Holyoke invented volleyball.

☐ Massachusetts takes its name from the Massachuset Indians, who once lived a few miles south of what is now Boston in an area known as Blue Hill. The tribe's name means "great hill."

☐ During the 1600s, Massachusetts Puritans (members of a strict religious group) made it a crime to celebrate Christmas, to dance at weddings, to perform religious music, to put on plays, and to wear buttons, lace, or shoe buckles.

☐ U.S. paper money is printed on paper made from a secret formula at the Crane & Company mill in Dalton, Massachusetts.

Horses graze on a farm in western Massachusetts.

A Trip Around the State

Massachusetts is a small state. In fact, 70 states the size of Massachusetts could fit inside Alaska, the country's largest state. But Massachusetts makes up for its size with a great variety of landscapes and natural attractions.

Massachusetts is bordered on the north by Vermont and New Hampshire. New York lies to the west, while Connecticut and Rhode Island share the southern border. To the east, beyond Massachusetts Bay, is the Atlantic Ocean. The many bays along the Atlantic coast of Massachusetts have earned the state its nickname—the Bay State.

Thousands of years ago, powerful mountains of moving ice called **glaciers** helped form the landscape of Massachusetts. As they slowly traveled across the region, the glaciers scoured the tops of mountains and dumped rocks, clay, and sand in low-lying areas.

9

Cape Cod National Seashore is a great place to collect rocks and seashells.

The glaciers also left rolling hills called **drumlins**. The drumlins are part of the Coastal Lowland—one of Massachusetts's four main land regions. Glaciers also shaped the valleys and hills of Massachusetts's other regions—the Eastern Upland, the Connecticut Valley Lowland, and the Western Upland.

The Coastal Lowland stretches inland from the seashore. Hundreds of small lakes and ponds dot this region, where pitch pines and scrub oaks grow. Sandy beaches line Massachusetts Bay and Cape Cod, a narrow **peninsula** that juts into the Atlantic Ocean. Across Nantucket Sound lie Nantucket, Martha's Vineyard, and many smaller islands.

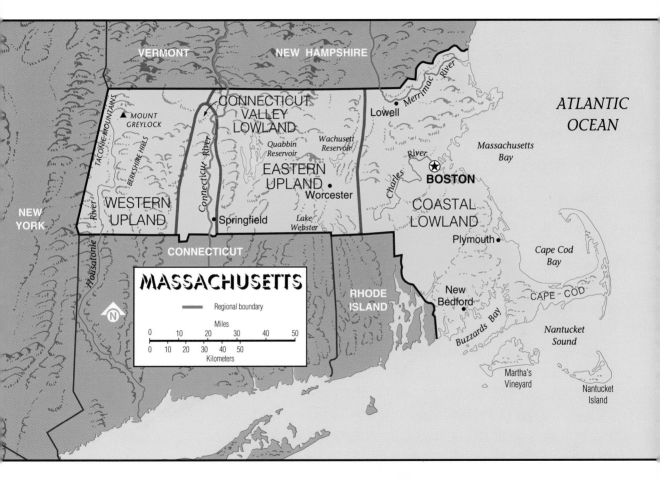

VERMONT

NEW HAMPSHIRE

ATLANTIC OCEAN

CONNECTICUT VALLEY LOWLAND

Lowell •

Merrimac River

▲ MOUNT GREYLOCK

TACONIC MOUNTAINS

BERKSHIRE HILLS

Connecticut River

Quabbin Reservoir

Wachusett Reservoir

Massachusetts Bay

River

⊛ **BOSTON**

EASTERN UPLAND • Worcester

Charles

WESTERN UPLAND

• Springfield

Lake Webster

COASTAL LOWLAND

NEW YORK

River

CONNECTICUT

Housatonic

Plymouth •

Cape Cod Bay

RHODE ISLAND

New Bedford •

CAPE • COD

MASSACHUSETTS

—— Regional boundary

Nantucket Sound

Miles

0   10   20   30   40   50

0   10   20   30   40   50

Kilometers

Ⓝ

Buzzards Bay

Martha's Vineyard

Nantucket Island

Azaleas

The land rises to elevations of 1,000 feet (300 meters) and higher in the Eastern Upland. Streams have cut narrow valleys through the hills of this region, which covers about half of Massachusetts. Stands of birch, beech, and pine trees flourish here, along with flowers such as marsh marigolds, bloodroots, and azaleas.

To the west, the land gradually slopes downward to the narrow Connecticut Valley Lowland, which follows the banks of the Connecticut River. The soil here is fertile, making the Connecticut Valley an important agricultural region. Farmers in the valley raise fruit, corn, and livestock.

Pastures *(above)* **and croplands** *(left)* **cover much of the Connecticut Valley Lowland.**

13

The Western Upland stretches from the Connecticut Valley Lowland to the bordering state of New York. Within the Western Upland are the Taconic Mountains and the Berkshire Hills. Mount Greylock, the highest spot in Massachusetts, rises 3,491 feet (1,064 m) in the Berkshire Hills.

Several major rivers—including the Connecticut, Charles, Merrimac, Housatonic, and Hoosic—flow through Massachusetts. At several places, river dams have been built to collect water in **reservoirs** (artificial lakes). Two of the largest reservoirs—Quabbin and Wachusett—supply drinking water to the city of Boston.

The climate of Massachusetts is typical of the northeastern United

Sugar maples, which thrive throughout Massachusetts, turn bright red and yellow in the fall.

States. Summers are usually warm and humid, and both rain and snow fall in the winter. But the weather varies from one region of Massachusetts to the next.

During the winter, mild ocean winds blow inland, raising temperatures in the Coastal Lowland. This region is also the warmest during the summer, while the Eastern Upland is the coolest. The Western Upland, the farthest region from the sea, is the coldest during the winter.

Summers on Martha's Vineyard are warm and sunny.

Each winter, snow blankets Massachusetts's fields and forests *(left)*, where bobcats *(below)* prowl for food.

January temperatures in the state average 25° F (–4° C). In July the average is 71° F (22° C). The lowest temperature ever recorded was –34° F (–37° C), and the highest was 107° F (42° C). Rainfall, which is generally heavier in the east, ranges from 38 to 48 inches (97 to 122 centimeters). The mountains of western Massachusetts receive the most snow—up to 75 inches (191 cm) a year.

Plentiful **precipitation** (rain and melted snow) allows thick forests to thrive in many parts of the state. Birch, beech, maple, and oak trees grow in the uplands, while pines and other evergreen trees are common along the coast. Marsh grasses favor the sandy soil of the Coastal Lowland.

The forests of Massachusetts are home to many animals. Rabbits, bobcats, deer, and foxes roam the uplands. The streams of the Western Upland shelter muskrat and beavers. Birds such as pheasant and partridge nest in fields and forests throughout the state. The beaches and harbors of the Atlantic coast attract terns, gulls, and other seabirds.

Massachusetts's Story

Native American peoples, or Indians, have lived in what is now Massachusetts for at least 3,000 years. The Algonquians, a group of many different Native American nations, settled much of eastern North America. Algonquian peoples in Massachusetts included the Nipmuc, Nauset, Pennacook, and Wampanoag.

The Algonquians hunted deer and beavers and grew crops—including corn, beans, and squash—in fertile land near rivers. They built canoes from birch bark and sewed their clothing from buckskin (deer hides). Algonquian homes, called wigwams, had frames made of strong wooden poles, which were covered by bark or animal skins. The wigwams provided a warm shelter during the winter.

Algonquians lived in wigwams *(left)* and hunted deer *(below)* for their meat and hides. One group of hunters chased their prey between two hedges, or fences, that narrowed at one end. The trapped deer made easy targets for another group of hunters waiting at the narrow end with bows and arrows.

The lives of the Algonquian peoples changed in the early 1600s, when European sea captains began exploring the shores of Cape Cod and the mainland of what is now Massachusetts. The Europeans brought with them deadly diseases, such as smallpox, that killed thousands of Indians along the Atlantic coast.

In 1620 a group of 102 people left Great Britain. Called **Pilgrims,** they were seeking the freedom to establish their own church. They boarded the *Mayflower* and set sail for Virginia, a British **colony** (settlement) along the Atlantic coast of North America.

After a long sea voyage, the *Mayflower* strayed off course and anchored off the shores of Cape Cod.

The *Mayflower*'s voyage across the Atlantic Ocean lasted 65 days.

A small landing party went ashore to explore the peninsula but found that the soil was too poor to farm. The *Mayflower* later sailed across Cape Cod Bay.

The settlers landed on the western shore of the bay, where they found good soil, plentiful game, and a safe harbor. The *Mayflower*'s passengers decided to stay and build a new colony, which they named Plymouth.

The Pilgrims had to get used to the chilly, snowy winter climate in their new land.

The Pilgrims were hardworking, but they knew little about farming and were unprepared for their new life at Plymouth Colony. Fewer than 60 of the settlers survived the first winter, partly because they didn't store enough food. Without the help of two Native Americans, Samoset and Squanto, the colony probably would have failed.

Squanto taught the Pilgrims how to plant corn, where to fish and hunt, and which plants were safe to use as food or medicine. Samoset introduced the Pilgrims to Massasoit, the sachem (great chief) of the Wampanoag Indians.

Soon after their first meeting, Massasoit and the Pilgrims signed a peace **treaty** (agreement) that would last more than 50 years. The Pilgrims and the Wampanoag promised not to harm each other. Anyone breaking the treaty would be sent to their own people for punishment.

To thank the Indians for their help, the Pilgrims invited them to a harvest feast. The feast, held in November 1621, marked the Pilgrims' first anniversary at Plymouth. The celebration lasted three days and became the first Thanksgiving in America.

When the Pilgrims met Samoset in 1621, they were surprised to discover that he spoke their language. Samoset had learned some English from British fishers on the coast of what is now Maine.

During the 1620s, new settlers arrived in Plymouth Colony. Some moved on to begin smaller settlements in Quincy, Salem, and Watertown. In 1630 a group of **Puritans** led by John Winthrop arrived in Salem. Like the Pilgrims, the Puritans were seeking religious freedom.

The British king had given the Puritans permission to begin a new colony near Plymouth. Soon after landing in Salem, the Puritans founded the city of Boston, which became the capital of their colony— Massachusetts Bay Colony. Near Boston some of the newcomers founded Harvard, the oldest college in North America. The colony grew at the rate of 1,000 settlers a year for the next 10 years.

Before setting sail for America, the Puritans elected John Winthrop to be their governor.

The success of the Puritans, however, became the misfortune of the Native Americans. The Puritans seized land without paying for it and made Indians obey the strict Puritan laws. As early as 1637, fighting broke out between the Puritans and the Wampanoag tribe.

The conflict over land led to King Philip's War, which broke out in 1675. After several bloody battles, the war ended in the defeat of the Wampanoag and in the death of their leader, Metacomet. With much of their land occupied by European settlers, the Wampanoag fled.

At the same time, thousands of new settlers arrived to work on the ships and in the harbors of Plymouth and Massachusetts Bay. As their economies grew, the people of the two colonies found that they had common interests and goals. In 1691 the British king and queen, William and Mary, allowed them to form a new colony called Massachusetts, which combined Massachusetts Bay and Plymouth colonies.

Metacomet, called King Philip by the British colonists, was killed in a battle against settlers in 1676.

Trouble Brews in Salem

In 1692 Salem Village was a quiet, rural community near the busy port of Salem. But late in the year, strange events began happening in the village. Frightened by tales of West Indian voodoo, several young women began to suffer frightening fits and visions. Suspecting that witchcraft was at work, the young women accused a West Indian woman in Salem of casting spells on them.

Soon the entire village was taking sides in the case. Samuel Parris, a minister from Salem Village, led the witch-hunt. Parris and his followers accused dozens of people of practicing witchcraft. Even the wife of William Phips, the governor of the colony, came under suspicion.

A special court in Salem convicted and hanged 19 people as witches. Giles Corey, a man who refused to plead either innocent or guilty, was pressed to death with heavy stones. A total of 150 people went to jail. But soon the people of Massachusetts turned against the witch trials, realizing that the accusations were false. In October Governor Phips ended the trials and released all suspected witches from prison.

During the 1700s, Britain forced the colonists in North America to pay heavy taxes to support the British army. Angered, some people in Massachusetts called for independence from Britain. But the British earned a lot of money from their colonies and did not want to give them up. To maintain order, the British government sent soldiers to Massachusetts.

Protests in Massachusetts and in other North American colonies grew violent. On March 5, 1770, a squad of British Redcoats (soldiers named for their bright red uniforms) opened fire on a crowd in Boston, killing five colonists. The colonists called this event the Boston Massacre.

An engraving of the Boston Massacre shows British soldiers firing on a crowd. The picture convinced many people to join in a rebellion against British rule.

In 1773 several citizens of Boston dumped 342 chests of British tea into Boston Harbor. After this event, called the Boston Tea Party, the British sent more troops and passed laws to punish the colonists.

In 1775 volunteer soldiers from the colonies clashed with the British army in the Massachusetts towns of Concord and Lexington. When they fired on the British troops, the colonists sparked the American Revolution. The next year, 13 of Britain's North American colonies, including Massachusetts, declared their independence.

On a cold December night in 1773, colonists disguised as Indians boarded three British ships in Boston Harbor and dumped hundreds of crates of tea into the water. The Boston Tea Party was a protest against the high taxes Britain charged on tea.

The True Story of the Midnight Ride

By 1775 the colony of Massachusetts was ready to fight the British. Determined to keep control, the British general Thomas Gage ordered his forces to march on the Massachusetts towns of Lexington and Concord. On April 18, 700 British Redcoats set out from Boston.

A Boston silversmith named Paul Revere found out about the mission and decided to act. At 10:00 that night, Revere and a friend, William Dawes, set out for Lexington to warn rebel leaders that the British were coming. At midnight the colonists reached

Lexington, where Dr. Samuel Prescott joined them. But before Revere and Dawes could reach Concord, the British arrested the two men. Only Dr. Prescott made it past the British patrols.

Thanks to Samuel Prescott, the rebels at Concord were ready for the Redcoats. But Prescott was forgotten after Henry Wadsworth Longfellow, a Massachusetts writer, penned "Paul Revere's Ride" in 1863. Because of this poem, the Boston silversmith—not Samuel Prescott—went down in history as the hero of the midnight ride.

In Cambridge, Massachusetts, General George Washington took command of the colonial forces, known as the Continental Army. In 1776 Washington forced British troops out of Boston. He led the Continental Army until 1783, when Britain agreed to a peace treaty and withdrew the Redcoats from the colonies.

The colonists then formed their own country—the United States of America. They wrote a **constitution** that explained how the new government would work. When Massachusetts approved the constitution of the United States in 1788, it became the sixth state to join the new union.

One year later, General Washington became the nation's first president. Voters elected John Adams of Massachusetts as the second president in 1796. John Quincy Adams, his son, would become the sixth president in 1825.

As the young country grew, so did shipping in Massachusetts. Trading vessels carried the state's goods to nations all over the world. Ships also sailed from the Massachusetts ports of New Bedford and Fall River to hunt whales for their fat, which was made into a valuable lamp oil. In the early 1800s, France and other European countries became important trading partners for Massachusetts.

Whale hunters from Massachusetts often risked their lives to chase down and kill the enormous animals.

At the same time, Britain and the United States were in conflict. Britain, which was at war with France, was trying to prevent Americans from trading with the French. The British were also searching U.S. ships and forcing U.S. sailors into the British navy. This led to war between the United States and Britain in 1812.

Although it ended quickly, the War of 1812 prevented Massachusetts from buying or selling its goods in Europe. As a result, the state had to start making its own products and soon became a pioneer in manufacturing.

In 1814 Francis Cabot Lowell built a cotton mill in the town of Waltham. The new textile mill was the first in the United States to combine all the operations needed to turn raw cotton into finished cloth. After Lowell's death, his business partners built an entire city of mills—called Lowell—on the banks of the Merrimac River north of Boston.

Companies in Lowell and in other Massachusetts cities made clothing, shoes, furniture, artificial limbs, musical instruments, and clipper ships. People seeking good wages and a better life moved from farms into the cities to work in the new factories.

Francis Cabot Lowell helped establish Massachusetts as a leader in manufacturing.

As the state's economy grew, **immigrants** from poor European countries arrived to look for jobs. Between 1846 and 1856, more than 1,000 Irish newcomers settled in Boston every month. By 1860 the state's population had topped 1 million.

Many of the European newcomers in Massachusetts took jobs in the state's busy textile (cloth) mills.

The House on Walden Pond

In 1845 a young writer from Concord named Henry David Thoreau began making plans to build a house. The house would be small and plain, but it would satisfy his need for shelter and comfort. Thoreau decided to build the house on the shores of Walden Pond, in the outskirts of Concord.

Thoreau wrote about his experience in *Walden; or, Life in the Woods.* In the book, he claimed that modern, fast-paced society made people unhappy, even desperate. But the simple life at Walden Pond offered something different— peace of mind. *Walden* has fascinated millions of readers since it first appeared in 1854.

With a growing audience for books and newspapers, publishing boomed in Massachusetts. William Lloyd Garrison of Boston produced a newspaper called *The Liberator*. In his articles, Garrison called for an end to slavery, a common practice in Southern states. (Massachusetts had already outlawed slavery.) Garrison and many citizens of Massachusetts and other Northern states helped runaway slaves escape from the South.

In 1861 conflicts between the Southern slaveholding states and the Northern free states led to the Civil War. The industries of the North became an important part of the war effort. Massachusetts supplied Northern troops with ships, clothing, and weapons. In addition, more than 14,000 soldiers from Massachusetts were killed or wounded while fighting for the North. The South surrendered in 1865.

More than 145,000 soldiers from Massachusetts fought for the North during the Civil War.

After the war, industry continued to grow in Massachusetts. Immigrants from Italy, Portugal, Germany, Poland, and many other countries worked in the mills and factories. But the workdays were long and the pay was low. Many workers earned only 85 cents for a 12-hour day. Women and children earned even less.

To protest against these conditions, many laborers joined unions (workers' organizations) in the early 1900s. When the unions called a strike, the workers stayed home from their jobs. The strikes forced business owners to either pay better wages or shut down their factories. The unions also persuaded

In 1912 state police met face-to-face with striking workers in Lawrence, Massachusetts.

Massachusetts to pass new laws controlling the hours and pay for workers.

A Sticky Situation

On January 15, 1919, one of the strangest floods in history nearly destroyed the city of Boston. That was the day of the Great Molasses Flood. A huge steel tank holding more than two million gallons (eight million liters) of molasses suddenly burst. The sweet, sticky wave poured through the city, destroying everything in its path.

When the flood of molasses finally came to a halt, a layer of goo three feet (one meter) thick covered much of Boston. In all, 21 people died in the flood, and at least 50 more were badly hurt. The smell of molasses lasted for months. Some people claim that, on hot days, the scent of molasses still lingers in the Boston air.

In the early 1900s, poorly paid factory workers lived in crowded, unclean neighborhoods.

During World War I (1914–1918), factories in Massachusetts turned out supplies for the U.S. armed forces. But the state's economy slumped in the 1920s. Massachusetts's companies could not compete with Southern businesses, which paid workers lower wages so they could make and sell goods more cheaply. As a result, Massachusetts had a hard time selling its higher-priced products. Many factories closed, and thousands of workers lost their jobs.

Conditions worsened during the Great Depression, which began in 1929. This economic crisis forced thousands of companies and banks throughout the nation to go out of business. In the worst years of the depression, almost half of all workers in Massachusetts were jobless.

The economy improved when the United States entered World War II in 1941. Factories in

When U.S. troops left to fight in World War II, many women in Massachusetts went to work making weapons.

Massachusetts again supplied weapons, and the state's shipyards turned out military vessels. But after the war ended in 1945, many of the state's remaining shoe and textile companies moved to the South.

At the same time, scientists in Massachusetts were developing computers and other new products. In the 1950s and 1960s, high-tech electronics companies started up near Boston. Researchers and engineers at the Massachusetts Institute of Technology (MIT) and other universities in the Boston area played an important part in the explosion of high-tech industry. The industry grew rapidly and created thousands of well-paying jobs.

10,000 B.C. A.D.1620 **1675** **1691** **1770 1775 1788**

Native Americans settle in what is now Massachusetts

Pilgrims arrive at Plymouth

King Philip's War erupts

British monarchs William and Mary grant a royal charter to the new colony of Massachusetts

Boston Massacre

The American Revolution begins with battles at Lexington and Concord

Massachusetts becomes the sixth state

Massachusetts continues to attract newcomers who seek a college education or who work in high-tech and manufacturing industries. Massachusetts's famous universities are training future engineers, computer designers, and business owners. With its talented workforce, the state has a promising future.

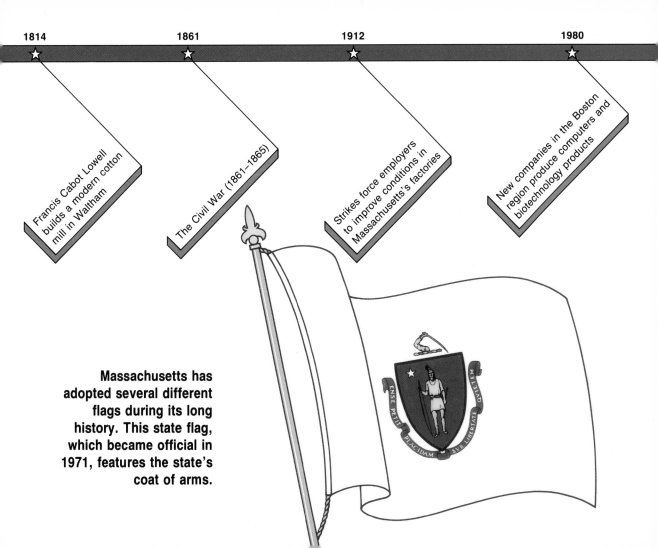

1814
Francis Cabot Lowell builds a modern cotton mill in Waltham

1861
The Civil War (1861–1865)

1912
Strikes force employers to improve conditions in Massachusetts's factories

1980
New companies in the Boston region produce computers and biotechnology products

Massachusetts has adopted several different flags during its long history. This state flag, which became official in 1971, features the state's coat of arms.

Children wearing costumes march in a New Year's Eve parade in Boston.

Living and Working in Massachusetts

People from all over the world have come to Massachusetts throughout its long history. Seeking religious freedom, the first British colonists built farms and ports near the seacoast. In the 1800s, Italian, Irish, and Portuguese immigrants worked on fishing boats or in factories. Nowadays, people of European descent make up about 88 percent of the state's population of 6 million.

Massachusetts is full of historical sites, such as this 200-year-old windmill on Nantucket Island.

Children in Worcester, Massachusetts, enjoy their summer vacation.

Before the Civil War, African Americans came to Massachusetts to escape slavery. Nowadays they represent 5 percent of the state's people. About the same number of Latinos, who come from Mexico and Central and South America, live in Massachusetts. Asian Americans, many of whom arrived after World War II, make up about 2 percent of the state's population. Native Americans, the area's first people, number only about 12,000— fewer than 1 percent.

About 8 out of every 10 residents of Massachusetts live in cities. Boston, the capital city, is the state's business and education center. Worcester, in central Massachusetts, and Springfield in the west are home to factories that produce machinery, textiles, and other manufactured goods. On Buzzards Bay, west of Cape Cod, lies the fishing port of New Bedford.

Boston

Although Boston is growing rapidly, many of the city's historical sites have been carefully preserved. Colonial mansions still line the bumpy brick streets of Beacon Hill. A two-story wooden house in the North End was once the home of Paul Revere, who warned colonists of a British invasion in 1775. Along the Black Heritage Trail are the homes, schools, and churches of African American Bostonians from the 1800s.

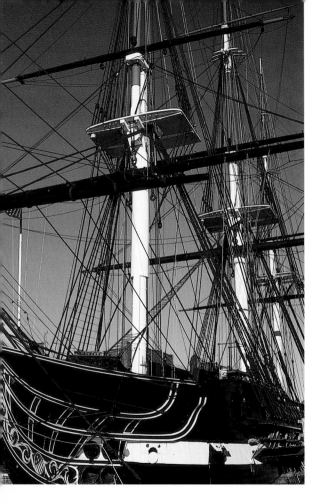

In the War of 1812, cannonballs bounced off the sturdy walls of the USS *Constitution,* earning the ship the nickname "Old Ironsides."

At the Charlestown Navy Yard, visitors tour the USS *Constitution,* the oldest warship in the U.S. Navy. Bostonians can relax and picnic on Boston Common—the nation's first public park—or see dolphins, sharks, and sea turtles at the New England Aquarium.

Massachusetts has preserved hundreds of its historic places. Plymouth Rock marks the site where the Pilgrims landed in 1620. The first battles of the American Revolution were fought at Lexington and at the Old North Bridge in Concord. Factories and mills in Lowell show the workings of a manufacturing town as it was in the early 1800s.

Outdoor enthusiasts hike and camp in Massachusetts's forests, which cover nearly two-thirds of the state. Every summer swimmers and sunbathers crowd Cape Cod National Seashore, with its 27,000 acres (11,000 hectares) of sand dunes, beaches, marshes, and woodlands. Adventuresome hikers follow the Appalachian Trail, which winds through the mountains of western Massachusetts on its way from Maine to Georgia.

Sun lovers flock to Sea Gull Beach in West Yarmouth, Massachusetts.

A batter for the Boston Red Sox gears up for the pitch.

As the birthplace of basketball, Massachusetts boasts the Boston Celtics, a longtime championship team. The Celtics and the Boston Bruins, a professional hockey team, play their games in Boston Garden. Visiting teams fear Fenway Park, the home of the Boston Red Sox and one of the country's oldest baseball stadiums.

The New England Patriots meet their professional football opponents in Foxboro, a few miles south of Boston. Every other year at Cambridge, Harvard University plays Yale University, a longtime football rival from Connecticut.

Students in Massachusetts benefit from an excellent educational system. Many scholars consider Harvard, the nation's oldest university, to be one of the best in the world. Future engineers and scientists study at MIT, a leading high-tech university that is also in Cambridge. College students in the town of Amherst attend Amherst College or the University of Massachusetts.

A young student *(top)* from North Andover, Massachusetts, takes a break from studying. About one million students attend Massachusetts's elementary and secondary schools. A college crew team *(left)* rows past Harvard University.

49

Workers harvest cranberries on Cape Cod.

Many college graduates remain in Massachusetts to pursue their careers. Most of the state's workers—75 percent—have jobs helping other people or businesses. These service workers include doctors, teachers, salespeople, lawyers, and bank tellers. Police officers, park rangers, and elected officials also have service jobs. The tourism industry, which earns Massachusetts $11 billion a year, employs hotel workers, travel agents, and tour guides. The state draws about 23 million visitors each year.

About 19 percent of Massachusetts's workers have jobs in manufacturing. Some factory workers still make shoes and fabrics. Others assemble machinery, sew clothing, process paper, or craft musical instruments. Workers at printing houses produce books, magazines, and newspapers. Skilled high-tech employees manufacture computers and robots.

While agriculture and fishing still earn money for Massachusetts, only 1 percent of the state's 3 million workers farm or fish. Massachusetts's farmers raise vegetables and dairy products and harvest about half of all the cranberries in the United States. Greenhouses in the state produce shrubs and garden plants.

About half of the scallops caught in the United States come from Massachusetts.

Fishing companies in Massachusetts haul in scallops, cod, haddock, and perch from the Atlantic Ocean. The largest fishing fleets sail from the ports of New Bedford and Gloucester.

But the state's fishing industry is growing smaller every year. Fishing companies are finding it more and more expensive to operate their fleets. In addition, flounder and other kinds of fish are fast disappearing because fishers have caught too many. Other fish have been poisoned by wastes dumped into rivers and harbors. Because of pollution, the state no longer allows commercial fishing boats to work in Boston Harbor, in Massachusetts Bay, and in other areas.

Workers fix and repaint an old fishing boat.

Protecting the Environment

Boston Harbor extends five miles (eight kilometers) out to Massachusetts Bay. The harbor has been an important part of Boston's economy for more than 300 years. But the rapid growth of the city has caused serious water pollution. Much more than tea has ended up in Boston Harbor, which is now one of the most polluted waterways in the United States.

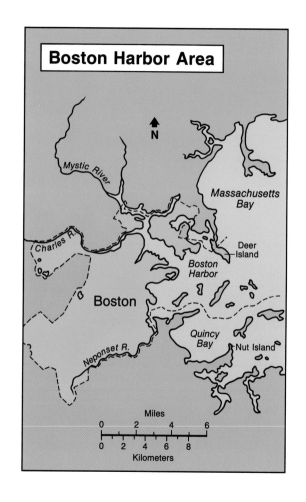

54

Tourism is important to businesses along Boston Harbor.

For many years, untreated sewage from Boston's homes and factories ran directly into the harbor's waters. Several rivers, including the Charles, Mystic, and Neponset, carried pollutants from other cities into the harbor.

In the mid-1900s, Boston built two sewage-treatment plants to remove poisonous bacteria from wastewater. But the plants proved unable to handle the rising flow of sewage. By the 1970s, more than 500 million gallons (1.9 billion

The Charles River, which flows through Boston, carries polluted water into Boston Harbor.

liters) of poorly treated wastewater were flowing into the harbor every day.

The bad-smelling water drove recreational boaters from the harbor. Tourists avoided the waterfront and swimmers stayed away from the filthy beaches, where untreated sewage was washing ashore. The polluted water also made the harbor's fish poisonous to eat. As many as 14,000 workers in the local fishing industry lost their jobs.

Although Boston built sewage-treatment plants on Deer Island (above) **and on Nut Island, the plants could not handle all the wastewater that flows into the harbor.**

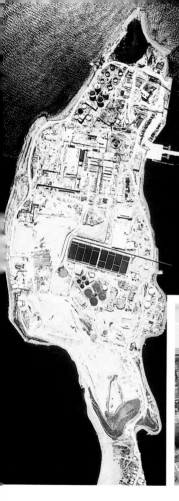

To solve the problem, state officials formed the Massachusetts Water Resources Authority (MWRA) in 1984. The MWRA planned to improve the old treatment plants and to build a new one on Deer Island, near the mouth of Boston Harbor. Until the plant opens in 1999, a 9-mile (14-km) outflow pipe will carry the city's untreated sewage out to Massachusetts Bay.

Many people want to stop the outflow pipe. They believe that the pipe should carry only treated sewage, which would be much less harmful

A new sewage-treatment plant *(near left)* **on Deer Island** *(far left),* **will help the old plant to better process wastewater.**

Above-water machines *(left)* **install sections of the outflow pipe. Under the water, workers construct the inside tunnels** *(below).*

to the waters of Massachusetts Bay. But the outflow pipe cannot carry treated sewage until the new plant on Deer Island is operating.

Many different types of ships use Boston Harbor.

The high costs of the new plant and of the outflow pipe have caused a fierce argument over who will have to pay for them. Some people say it is Boston's problem, so the city should pay. Others believe the rest of the state should help, because Boston Harbor is so important to the economy of all of Massachusetts.

If workers finish on schedule, the harbor will be cleaner by 1999. In the meantime, Massachusetts has learned that ignoring environmental problems only makes them more difficult to solve.

60

Swimmers compete in a race across Boston Harbor. As the water becomes cleaner, more people will enjoy swimming, boating, and fishing in the harbor.

Massachusetts's Famous People

ACTIVISTS

Susan B. Anthony (1820–1906) was a women's rights advocate born in Adams, Massachusetts. She fought hard to win women the right to vote, to control personal property, and to gain custody of their children after a divorce.

Crispus Attucks (1723?–1770), an African American resident of Boston, led a mob of colonists against a squad of British soldiers on March 5, 1770. Attucks was the first to fall as the Redcoats fired on the crowd.

William E. B. Du Bois (1868–1963) was a writer, educator, and civil rights leader. Born in Great Barrington, Massachusetts, he attended Harvard University and later edited *Crisis,* the magazine of the National Association for the Advancement of Colored People (NAACP).

▼ CRISPUS ATTUCKS

▲ W. E. B. DU BOIS

SUSAN B. ANTHONY ▶

▼ JANE ALEXANDER

▼ BETTE DAVIS

ACTORS

Jane Alexander (born 1939) won a Tony Award for her performance in the play *The Great White Hope.* This actress from Boston has also appeared in movies and television shows. In 1993 she became the head of the National Endowment for the Arts, a government agency that supports arts organizations.

Bette Davis (1908–1989), a native of Lowell, starred in dozens of films, earning two Academy Awards. Davis's talent and strong personality helped create better film roles for women. Among her best-known movies are *Whatever Happened to Baby Jane?* and *All About Eve.*

Jack Lemmon (born 1925), a well-known actor, was born in Boston. He starred in *The Odd Couple* and won Academy Awards for his work in *Mister Roberts* and *Save the Tiger*.

ATHLETE

Patricia Bradley (born 1951) is one of the most successful professional golfers in history. Originally from Westford, Massachusetts, Bradley has won more than $4 million on the Ladies Professional Golf Association tour.

ALEXANDER ▶
GRAHAM BELL

▼ ROBERT GODDARD

SUMNER REDSTONE ▶

BUSINESS LEADER & INVENTORS

Alexander Graham Bell (1847–1922) was born in Scotland but later moved to Boston, where he opened a school for teachers of the deaf. In 1876 Bell became the first person to send his voice over an electric wire. In the same year, he patented the first telephone.

Robert Goddard (1882–1945) dreamed of rockets, spacecraft, and trips to the moon as a young man. Raised in Worcester, Massachusetts, he launched the world's first liquid-fuel rocket in 1926.

Sumner Redstone (born 1923) is the chairman of Viacom, Inc., a large entertainment company that owns the cable channels MTV, Showtime, and Nickelodeon. A native of Boston, Redstone was the first theater operator to build multiplexes, where two or more movie screens operate under one roof.

COOK

Fannie Farmer (1857–1915) was the first cook to use standard measurements in food recipes. She founded a cooking school and wrote *The Boston Cooking School Cook Book*. First published in 1896, this book later became the *Fannie Farmer Cookbook*.

MUSICIANS & ARTISTS

Leonard Bernstein (1918–1990) was a composer and orchestral conductor best known for his musicals *West Side Story* and *Candide*. Born in Lawrence, Massachusetts, Bernstein introduced thousands of people to classical music through his lectures and television specials.

◀ **FANNIE FARMER**

LEONARD BERNSTEIN ▶

▲ **WINSLOW HOMER**

CHICK COREA ▶

Armando "Chick" Corea (born 1941) is a Grammy Award–winning musician from Chelsea, Massachusetts. A keyboard player and composer, Corea blends jazz, rock, classical, and other types of music in his performances.

Winslow Homer (1836–1910), an artist from Boston, taught himself how to paint as a young man. He produced illustrations of the Civil War for the magazine *Harper's Weekly*. He later settled in Prouts Neck, Maine. Homer's best-known works are his seascapes.

N. C. Wyeth (1882–1945) was an illustrator of children's novels. A native of Needham, Massachusetts, Wyeth used his great talent for drawing to illustrate books such as *Robin Hood* and *Treasure Island*.

John Adams (1735–1826) of Braintree (now Quincy), Massachusetts, was elected the second president of the United States in 1796. Adams was the first president to live in the White House in Washington, D.C.

Oliver Wendell Holmes, Jr. (1841–1935) practiced law in his hometown of Boston after serving in the Union army during the Civil War. Holmes served on the U.S. Supreme Court from 1902 until 1932 and became famous for teaching judges not to let their personal opinions influence their decisions in court.

John F. Kennedy (1917–1963), the 35th president of the United States, was born in Brookline, Massachusetts. The youngest president ever to be elected, he was assassinated in Dallas, Texas, on November 22, 1963.

JOHN ADAMS ▶

OLIVER
▼ WENDELL HOLMES

▲ JOHN F.
KENNEDY

WRITERS

Louisa May Alcott (1832–1888) moved with her family to Boston as a child. An author mainly of stories for young people, Alcott's most famous book is *Little Women*.

Theodore Seuss Geisel (1904–1991), also known as Dr. Seuss, wrote easy-to-read rhyming books about make-believe creatures. Millions of children have enjoyed *The Cat in the Hat* and many other books by Dr. Seuss, who was born in Springfield.

Edgar Allan Poe (1809–1849), who was born in Boston, wrote scary poems and stories that earned him a reputation as the nation's finest horror writer. His best-known stories include "The Tell-Tale Heart," "The Fall of the House of Usher," and the poem "The Raven."

▲ LOUISA MAY
ALCOTT

EDGAR ▲
ALLEN
POE

DR. SEUSS ▶

65

Facts-at-a-Glance

Nickname: Bay State
Song: "All Hail to Massachusetts"
Motto: *Ense Petit Placidam Sub Libertate Quietem*
(By The Sword We Seek Peace, But Peace Only Under Liberty)
Flower: mayflower
Tree: American elm
Bird: chickadee

Population: 6,016,425*
Rank in population, nationwide: 13th
Area: 10,555 sq mi (27,337 sq km)
Rank in area, nationwide: 44th
Date and ranking of statehood:
February 6, 1788, the 6th state
Capital: Boston
Major cities (and populations*): Boston (574,283), Worcester (169,759), Springfield (156,983), Lowell (103,439), New Bedford (99,922)
U.S. senators: 2
U.S. representatives: 10
Electoral votes: 12

*1990 census

Places to visit: Children's Museum and Museum of Science in Boston, Walden Pond in Concord, Whaling Museum in New Bedford, Plimoth Plantation in Plymouth, Witch House in Salem, Basketball Hall of Fame in Springfield, Cape Cod National Seashore on Cape Cod

Annual events: Boston Marathon (April), Cape Cod Chowder Festival (June), Sandcastle Contest in Nantucket (August), Rowing Regatta in Cambridge (October), First Night Celebration in Boston (New Year's Eve)

Natural resources: granite, limestone, marble, natural harbors, peat, sand and gravel, sandstone, water

Agricultural products: apples, cranberries, greenhouse plants, vegetables, milk, eggs

Manufactured goods: electrical equipment and supplies, nonelectric machinery, scientific instruments, computers, transportation equipment, books and newspapers

ENDANGERED SPECIES
Mammals—blue whale, fin whale, humpback whale, northern right whale, sperm whale
Birds—stormy petrel, bald eagle, peregrine falcon, sedge wren, short-eared owl, roseate tern, golden-winged warbler
Reptiles—bog turtle, copperhead, timber rattlesnake, Plymouth redbelly turtle
Plants—northeastern bulrush, mountain cranberry, spurred gentian, ram's head, lady's-slipper, northern prickly rose, winged monkey-flower, sand violet

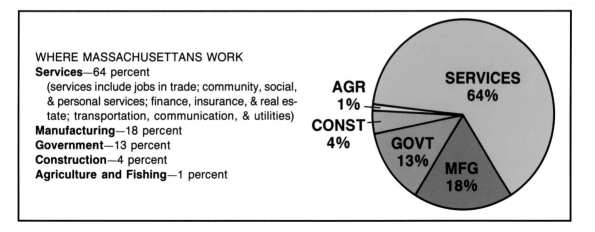

WHERE MASSACHUSETTANS WORK
Services—64 percent
   (services include jobs in trade; community, social, & personal services; finance, insurance, & real estate; transportation, communication, & utilities)
Manufacturing—18 percent
Government—13 percent
Construction—4 percent
Agriculture and Fishing—1 percent

AGR
1%
CONST
4%
GOVT
13%
MFG
18%
SERVICES
64%

PRONUNCIATION GUIDE

Algonquian (al-GAHN-kwee-uhn)

Amherst (AM-erst)

Berkshire (BERK-sher)

Housatonic (hoo-suh-TAHN-ihk)

Massachuset (mass-uh-CHOO-suht)

Massasoit (mass-uh-SOYT)

Nipmuc (NIHP-muhk)

Pennacook (PEHN-uh-kook)

Quabbin (KWAH-bihn)

Samoset (SAM-eh-set)

Taconic (tuh-KAHN-ihk)

Wampanoag (wahm-puh-NOH-ag)

Worcester (WUS-ter)

Glossary

colony A territory ruled by a country some distance away.

constitution The system of basic laws or rules of a government, society, or organization. The document in which these laws or rules are written.

drumlin A hill of rocks and earth moved into place by ancient glaciers.

glacier A large body of ice and snow that moves slowly over land.

immigrant A person who moves into a foreign country and settles there.

peninsula A stretch of land almost completely surrounded by water.

Pilgrim   One of the early English settlers who sailed to Massachusetts in
the 1600s. The Pilgrims were seeking
the freedom to practice their religion.

precipitation   Rain, snow, hail, and other
forms of moisture that fall to earth.

Puritan   A member of an English religious group that followed a strict form
of Christianity. Many Puritans left
Great Britain during the 1600s because
they were not allowed to practice their
religion there.

reservoir   A place where water is col-
lected and stored for later use.

treaty   An agreement between two or
more groups, usually having to do with
peace or trade.

Index

Acknowledgments

Maryland Cartographics, pp. 2, 11; Thomas P. Benincas, Jr., pp. 2–3, 47, 52; University Archives / Univ. of KS, p. 6; Jack Lindstrom, p. 7; Monica V. Brown, p. 8; Lynn M. Stone, p. 10; Root Resources: Louise K. Broman, p. 12, Lloyd & Mary McCarthy, p. 16, Jack Monsarratt, p. 50; Laatsch-Hupp Photo: Barbara Laatsch Hupp, pp. 12–13, 43, Lois E. Clarke, pp. 13, 19 (left), Donna L. Allen, pp. 14, 16, Virginia DiSabatino, pp. 45, 70, Jo DiMauro, pp. 49 (top), 55, © Kathleen Savage, p. 56, © Roslyn MacNish, p. 69; © Saul Mayer, p. 15; William S. Fowler / *Bulletin of the MA Archaeological Society*, p. 18; Reprinted with permission from *New England Indians*, © 1978 by C. Keith Wilber, The Globe Pequot Press, p. 19 (right); Library of Congress, pp. 20, 21, 25, 26, 28, 34 (inset), 36, 62 (top right), 63 (lower left), 65 (top left); Charles Hoffbauer, The New England, Boston, MA, pp. 23, 24, 29; The Bostonian Society / Old State House, pp. 27, 37; New Bedford Whaling Museum, p. 31; *Dictionary of American Portraits*, pp. 32, 63 (center), 65 (lower left); Museum of American Textile History, p. 33; © Judith Jango-Cohen, p. 34; Historic Northampton, pp. 35, 39; *The Lawrence Survey*, Coll. of Immigrant City Archives, p. 38; Ken Martin / Amstock, pp. 42, 44, 49 (bottom); © Eliot Cohen, p. 46; Boston Red Sox, p. 48; Tony LaGruth, p. 53; Kevin A. Kerwin / Regina Villa Assoc., pp. 57, 58 (left & right), 59 (left & right), 61; Mae Scanlan, p. 60; IPS, pp. 62 (top left & top center), 64 (top right); Martha Swope Photography, Nat'l. Endowment for the Arts, p. 62 (lower left); Hollywood Book & Poster, pp. 62 (lower right), 63 (top left); © Jeff Hornback, p. 63 (top right); Viacom, p. 63 (lower right); Fanny Farmer Candies, div. of Archibald Candy Corp., p. 64 (top left); Collections of the Maine Hist. Society, p. 64 (lower left); GRP Records, p. 64 (lower right); Independence Nat'l. Historical Park Coll., p. 65 (top center); John F. Kennedy Library, p. 65 (top right); Random House, p. 65 (lower center); Brown Univ. Library, p. 65 (lower right); Jean Matheny, p. 66.